PSALM PRAYERS
for the NATIONS

ENGAGE YOUR FAMILY WITH
40 SCRIPTURE-BASED PRAYERS

Sarah Keeling

Psalm Prayers for the Nations: Engage Your Family with 40 Scripture-Based Prayers

Copyright © 2020 by Sarah Keeling

All Rights Reserved

Cover and interior design: Typewriter Creative Co.
Copy editor: Barbara Coots

All rights reserved. No part of this publication may be reproduced, stored in a retrieval system, or transmitted in any form by any means, electronic, mechanical, photocopy, recording, or otherwise, without the prior permission of the publisher, except as provided for by USA copyright law.

Scripture quotations marked (CEV) are from the Contemporary English Version Copyright © 1991, 1992, 1995 by American Bible Society. Used by Permission.

Scripture quotations marked (CSB) have been taken from the Christian Standard Bible®, Copyright © 2017 by Holman Bible Publishers. Used by permission. Christian Standard Bible® and CSB® are federally registered trademarks of Holman Bible Publishers.

Scripture quotations marked (ESV) are from the ESV® Bible (The Holy Bible, English Standard Version®), copyright © 2001 by Crossway, a publishing ministry of Good News Publishers. Used by permission. All rights reserved.

Scripture quotations marked (ICB) are taken from The Holy Bible, International Children's Bible®. Copyright © 1986, 1988, 1999 by Thomas Nelson. Used by permission. All rights reserved.

Scripture quotations marked (NIV) are taken from the Holy Bible, New International Version®, NIV®. Copyright © 1973, 1978, 1984, 2011 by Biblica, Inc.® Used by permission of Zondervan. All rights reserved worldwide. www.zondervan.com. The "NIV" and "New International Version" are trademarks registered in the United States Patent and Trademark Office by Biblica, Inc.™

Scripture quotations marked (NLT) are taken from the Holy Bible, New Living Translation, copyright © 1996, 2004, 2015 by Tyndale House Foundation. Used by permission of Tyndale House Publishers, Inc., Carol Stream, Illinois 60188. All rights reserved.

ISBN: 978-1-7336016-1-0 (Paperback)
ISBN: 978-1-7336016-2-7 (eBook)

Published in the United States by Heart Work Tees

www.sarah-keeling.com

For our many friends around the world sacrificing much so that others may know Jesus,
Diuxi coo nda'ya' lii (God bless you).

CONTENTS

7

Introduction

11

Help for Families

15

Prayers

97

Letter of Gratitude

98

List of Contributors

101

About the Author

INTRODUCTION

For where two or three gather in my name,
there am I with them.

Matthew 18:20 (NIV)

Therefore go and make disciples of all nations...

Matthew 28:19a (NIV)

Dear Families,

As a mom, I tend to focus on my immediate family each day: wake the kids, take our older son to school, feed the baby, play with the baby, get the baby to nap, etc. I confess that I often forget that billions of people around the world are living hopeless, broken lives, desperate for salvation. People who have never heard about Jesus.

Obviously, I still need to take care of my family, but what if I could do something to help the unreached while waiting in the school pickup line or while we attempt a quick family dinner?

That's when I decided to compile these prayers for my family and your family, to help us do something together. Prayer is an underutilized, yet powerful weapon, especially when we are praying the Word of God.

We have been praying for our Bible translation friends in Oaxaca, Mexico, for several years as a family. When we had the opportunity to visit them and see how God had answered our prayers, our lives were forever changed. God has knit our hearts together with those of our Zapoteco del Istmo friends in ways we never thought possible.

It is incredibly special that we can be a part of what God is doing around the world without having to physically travel from our homes. I often forget the magnitude of such a gift — that God is accessible to us, and that our prayers are like a wonderful-smelling incense to Him (Revelation 5:8).

Forty families participated in writing the prayers for this book, which are meant to be read together as a family. Through Jesus, we come before God on his "throne of grace" (Hebrews 4:16) together, and God bends down to listen to our prayers (Psalm 116:2).

God has used our family prayer times to draw us closer to Himself and to each other. I hope your family will experience the same unification that our family has as we have prayed together.

I hope and pray this book will be a valuable resource to help families pray short, yet powerful prayers together for the many people around the world who have never heard about Jesus and the hope of salvation found in Him.

Blessings,

Sarah

HELP FOR FAMILIES

PARENT TIPS

Everyone is busy, but praying together as a family is time well spent. Each prayer is short and takes less than five minutes. Here are a few tips to easily incorporate this prayer time into your day:

- Start bedtime five minutes earlier each night to allow time to read a prayer.
- Place the book on your kitchen table, and read a prayer before dinner each evening.
- If your child can read, have him/her read a prayer on the way to school. If you have multiple children, let them take turns reading the prayers.
- Keep it simple. Something is better than nothing, and our children are absorbing more than we can see.
- Have realistic expectations, especially as you begin these prayers. Your children may not jump for joy at the thought of praying for the nations, and that is OK!

GO DEEPER

Since these prayers are short, you might want to extend the time with your children. Here are a few ideas for how to go deeper with your children using the prayers:

- Define the attributes of God used in the verses and prayers. Utilize resources such as Blue Letter Bible (www.blueletterbible.org).

- Ask your children, "What do you think that means?"

- Ask your children application questions based on the prayers, such as, "How have you experienced God's love?"

- Open your Bible and read the entire Psalm together.

- Using a Bible app, listen to the Psalm together.

- Have fun and be creative! There are endless possibilities that will help your kids get the most out of this family prayer experience.

GET PERSONAL

Each prayer is focused on one of the following areas: Bible translation, missionaries, pastors, and the unreached who have never heard about Jesus. Our family has discovered that we are much more personally impacted by our prayers when focusing on specific people. It seems like our prayers come alive when we pray for a real person in a real place.

Here are a few ways to help further connect your family with these prayer focuses:

- Highlight the specific prayer focus with your children and explain what role it plays in reaching the nations.

- Ask your children for their definition of each prayer focus and encourage them with more details.

- Select a specific unreached people group for your prayers.
    - Utilize resources such as Pray for Zero (www.prayforzero.com).
    - Sign up to adopt a Bibleless people group.

- Research your people group and provide related cultural experiences for your family.
    - Cook cultural meals.
    - Dress up in cultural clothes.
    - Act out cultural customs.

- Ask your church for resources about the missionaries it supports and ways to connect with them.
  - Host a family video call with missionaries.
  - Make a family video for the missionaries.
  - Study the location and culture where they are working and provide cultural information and experiences for your family.

PRAYERS

Sing to the LORD a new song;
sing to the LORD, all the earth.
Sing to the LORD, praise his name;
proclaim his salvation day after day.
Declare his glory among the nations,
his marvelous deeds among all peoples.

Psalm 96:1-3 (NIV)

DAY 1

THE KEELING FAMILY

But you are my shield,

and you give me victory

and great honor.

I pray to you, and you answer

from your sacred hill.

Psalm 3:3-4 (CEV)

PRAISES

God, You are our shield.

You are victorious.

You are full of honor.

You are sacred.

THANKS

God, thank You for shielding Bible translators
from danger around the world.

Thank You that You give Your people victory and honor.

Thank You that You hear our prayers and
answer us from Your sacred holy hill.

REQUESTS

God, please continue to shield and protect Bible
translators, especially in hostile areas.

Please provide victory and honor to the translation teams.

Please hear the translators' prayers and
answer them from Your sacred hill.

In Jesus' name,

Amen

DAY 2

THE BAKER FAMILY

"Be still, and know that I am God!
I will be honored by every nation.
I will be honored throughout the world."
The LORD of Heaven's Armies is here among us;
the God of Israel is our fortress.

Psalm 46:10-11 (NLT)

PRAISES

Lord God, You are the King of the nations,
You are the King over the whole earth.

There is no place on earth that Your glory does not fill.

You are exalted above every other god, and it
is to Your name that we give our praise.

THANKS

Lord, thank You for reminding pastors to be still, rest from
their work, and take time to know that You are God.

Thank You that the exaltation of Your Name among
Bibleless peoples is not dependent on pastors'
or people's efforts, but on Your efforts.

Thank You that when pastors take the time to
be still and remember who You are, Your Name
is exalted in all places on the earth.

REQUESTS

Lord, in the work of Bible translation, it is easy
to feel like the work is up to us to do.

But really, it is the work of Your Spirit that causes
Your Word to be exalted in all the earth.

Please remind pastors, who work to sow the good
seed of Your Word in the hearts of the Bibleless
peoples, that their job is to trust You, to wait upon Your
timing, to follow and obey Your Word, and that You
will cause Your Name to be known to all peoples.

Please give rest to their weary hearts, please give
strength to their weary hands, and please lift their eyes
up and out to You to see Your glory in all the earth.

In Jesus' Name we pray,

Amen

DAY 3

THE SCHMIDT FAMILY

The LORD is compassionate and gracious,
slow to anger and abounding in faithful love.

Psalm 103:8 (CSB)

PRAISES

Lord God, You are unconditionally loving.

You are forgiving.

You are polite.

You are always concerned for us.

You are calm.

THANKS

Lord God, thank You that You equip Your leaders
to spread the good news all around the world.

Thank You that we do not have to
depend on merely ourselves.

Thank You that Your love for us is constant and plentiful.

Thank You for working through us to spread Your love.

REQUESTS

Lord God, please allow our missionaries to be like You.

Please give them unconditional love and
patience while on the mission fields.

Please give them gentle spirits that are contagious
and create wonder to unbelievers.

Please use them to honor You and transform lives forever.

In Jesus' name,

Amen

DAY 4

THE BEAVERS FAMILY

The Lord is my light and the one who saves me.

So why should I fear anyone?

The Lord protects my life.

So why should I be afraid?

Psalm 27:1 (ICB)

PRAISES

God, You are our light and song.

You are our redeemer.

You are protection and peace.

God, You alone are our comfort and salvation.

THANKS

God, our precious redeemer, thank You for protection over our missionaries around the world.

Thank You that You are their song and the light that guides their way.

Thank You for the strength, comfort, and peace that allows them to go on.

REQUESTS

God, we ask in Your powerful name to protect missionaries in every nation.

May they feel strengthened by Your peace.

We ask You to consume their hearts and minds so that there will be no fear.

Please save and redeem a multitude of lives through the passion our missionaries have to see this lost world saved.

In Jesus' name,

Amen

DAY 5

THE WILLIS FAMILY

O LORD, our Lord, your majestic name fills the earth!
Your glory is higher than the heavens.

Psalm 8:1 (NLT)

PRAISES

God, You are magnificent.

You are excellent.

You are worthy.

You are glorious,

You are mighty!

THANKS

God, thank You for filling the earth with Your glory.

Thank You for filling the earth with many Bibles.

Thank You for the translators who diligently work to translate Bibles into different languages.

REQUESTS

God, please protect Bible translators as they attempt to fill the earth with Bibles in every person's heart language.

For every person who receives the Scriptures in their heart language, make Yourself known to them in a personal way, so that they can see Your glory has been around them all along.

May Your name fill the earth in every person's heart language!

In Jesus' name,

Amen

DAY 6

THE JOHNSON FAMILY

Live under the protection

of God Most High

and stay in the shadow

of God All-Powerful.

Then you will say to the Lord,

"You are my fortress,

my place of safety;

you are my God,

and I trust you."

Psalm 91:1-2 (CEV)

PRAISES

El Shaddai, as we work to spread Your Truth to the nations, we praise You as our Protector.

You are an Omnipotent Fortress, a refuge of safety.

We praise You as You cover us with Your wings, and in Your shadow we stay and rest.

As our Promise-Keeper, we can trust You.

THANKS

We thank You, Yahweh, for your shield of protection as workers navigate dangerous territories and bring light to a dark place.

You bring wisdom to them as they seek You and follow Your path.

Thank You for leading them to unreached lands so they may be used by You to make your name known.

Thank You for Your Word and the promises You keep.

REQUESTS

Help Your workers' hearts to continue to pursue You and Your right path.

Continue to lead them where they will glorify You most.

Protect them in the dark places as they shine Your light onto others.

We ask that You would show them the way to teach people that You can be trusted, that You are good and that You provide a peace that surpasses all understanding.

Your safety comes from the Hope we have in You as our Creator and Covenant-Keeper. We love You.

In Jesus' name,

Amen

DAY 7

THE REAVES FAMILY

For the LORD is good, and his faithful love endures forever;

his faithfulness, through all generations.

Psalm 100:5 (CSB)

PRAISES

God, You are so very good.

You are loving.

You are faithful.

You are forever.

THANKS

God, thank You for the goodness of Your ways with our missionaries.

Thank You for Your love and Your faithfulness to those who do Your will.

Thank You for Your promise of eternity.

REQUESTS

God, please make our missionaries examples of Your goodness.

Please empower them to show Your love and Your faithfulness to those whom they serve.

Please help them share the message of Your eternal love.

In Jesus' name,

Amen

DAY 8

THE DEMENT FAMILY

The LORD is my strength and my song;

he has become my salvation.

Psalm 118:14 (CSB)

PRAISES

God, You are our strength.

You are our saving grace.

You are worthy of praise.

You are merciful to us.

THANKS

God, thank You for empowering pastors and working through them to reach the lost and hurting.

Thank You for calling men and women to disciple others, to lead them in their faith and to teach them to praise and worship You.

Thank You for salvation, and that the message of the Gospel can be spread as a result of the love and dedication of pastors across the globe.

REQUESTS

God, please continue to empower pastors working among the unreached, enabling them to keep learning, growing and teaching so that others will see God through them.

Please protect pastors from growing weary or discouraged in their work. May they see lives changed and be fulfilled while giving all glory to God.

God, we pray for Your kingdom to grow and the message of salvation to spread as a result of the work of these pastors of the unreached.

In Jesus' name,

Amen

DAY 9

THE MENN FAMILY

But the Lord rules forever.

He sits on his throne to judge.

The Lord will judge the world by what is right.

He will decide what is fair for the nations.

Psalm 9:7-8 (ICB)

PRAISES

God, You rule forever!

You are high and lifted up!

God, You are the righteous judge of all creation.

THANKS

Thank You that You are the highest King who protects missionaries around the world.

Thank You, God, that You have called Your people to be missionaries and that You give them all they need.

REQUESTS

God, please protect those You have called, so that they can continue to do Your will.

Please continue to be the righteous judge who thwarts the enemy's plans against Your people who are called as missionaries.

In Jesus' name,

Amen

DAY 10

THE FERGUSON FAMILY

It is wonderful to be grateful
and to sing your praises,
LORD Most High!
It is wonderful each morning
to tell about your love
and at night to announce
how faithful you are.

Psalm 92:1-2 (CEV)

PRAISES

You are our Lord Most High.

You are Love.

You are Faithful.

You are worthy of our praise.

THANKS

Thank You for loving us unconditionally.

Thank You for always hearing our prayers.

Thank You for giving us Your Word as our Truth to guide us.

REQUESTS

Lord, please help Your followers throughout the world to show Your love to others daily.

Lord, let Bible translators feel Your presence today.

God, we pray for their friends and families who do not yet know You, that their eyes will be open to Your love, faithfulness, and truth.

In Jesus' name,

Amen

DAY 11

THE DEYTON FAMILY

You are my hiding place; you protect me from trouble.
You surround me with joyful shouts of deliverance.

Psalm 32:7 (CSB)

PRAISES

God, You are my hiding place.

You are safe.

You are my Protector.

You surround me in safety.

You deliver me.

THANKS

God, thank You for being a safe place for me and others around the world to hide when there is trouble.

Thank You God for protecting Your people in dangerous places.

Thank You for surrounding Bible translators right now with songs of freedom and deliverance.

REQUESTS

God, please continue to be the only true hiding place of safety for those in dangerous areas doing Your work.

Please provide protection from all types of trouble encountered by translation teams throughout the world.

Please keep surrounding all those who love You with songs of freedom and deliverance.

In Jesus' Name,

Amen

DAY 12

THE FAUGHT FAMILY

Blessed be the LORD God, the God of Israel,

who alone does wonders.

Blessed be his glorious name forever;

the whole earth is filled with his glory.

Amen and amen.

Psalm 72:18-19 (CSB)

PRAISES

God, I praise You because You alone work wonders.

I praise You because Your name is glorious.

I praise You because the whole earth is filled with Your glory.

THANKS

God, thank You for calling and sending missionaries
to people who do not know You.

Thank You that You give missionaries the words
to tell people about Your glorious name.

Thank You for helping missionaries to make
Your glory known in the whole earth.

REQUESTS

God, please give missionaries a passion to share Your wonders
with people who have never heard the good news before.

Please give missionaries boldness to make
Your glorious name known to the world.

Please help missionaries glorify You in everything
they do so that people can see You in them.

In Jesus' name,

Amen and amen

DAY 13

THE DABNEY FAMILY

The Lord guards you.

The Lord protects you as the shade protects you from the sun.

The sun cannot hurt you during the day.

And the moon cannot hurt you at night.

Psalm 121:5-6 (ICB)

PRAISES

God, You are our guardian.

God, You are our protection.

God, You provide shade for us.

THANKS

God, thank You for guarding missionaries around the world who are sharing Your good news.

God, thank You for protecting missionaries from harm.

God, thank You for being the shade, the sunscreen, that keeps missionaries safe.

REQUESTS

God, we pray for You to guard missionaries from political danger.

God, we pray for Your continued protection for missionaries who are in places where they face physical danger.

God, we pray for You to shade missionaries from the schemes of the enemy who looks to harm them and prevent them from sharing Jesus with the world.

In Jesus' name,

Amen

DAY 14

THE ELAM FAMILY

But I, through the abundance of your steadfast love,

will enter your house.

I will bow down toward your holy temple

in the fear of you.

Lead me, O LORD, in your righteousness

because of my enemies;

make your way straight before me.

Psalm 5:7-8 (ESV)

PRAISES

Praise you, LORD, that You are full of lovingkindness.

You are Holy.

You are Righteous.

THANKS

LORD, thank You that Your abundant lovingkindness
allows us to enter into Your house to worship.

Thank You for Your willingness to lead us in righteousness.

Thank You for making our paths straight
when we don't know which way to go.

REQUESTS

LORD, we pray on behalf of those who do not
have the Bible in their own heart language.

LORD, there is so much work to be done, money to be raised,
and people needed who are willing to sacrifice for them.

Would You lead them and us in your righteousness and
straighten every path that leads to them knowing You?

In Jesus' name,

Amen

DAY 15

THE PERRY FAMILY

Let all that I am praise the Lord.
O LORD my God, how great you are!
You are robed with honor and majesty.
You are dressed in a robe of light.
You stretch out the starry curtain of the heavens...

Psalm 104:1-2 (NLT)

PRAISES

God, You are worthy to be praised.

You are great. You are honor, and You are majesty.

You are clothed in light, there is no one else like You.

You created the Heavens and all that is in them.

You stretched out the heavens as if that were nothing.

THANKS

Father, thank You for freely giving us
the opportunity to know You.

Knowing You gives us purpose for our lives.

Our purpose is to bring praise to You and Your great name.

Thank You for the salvation we receive through knowing You.

REQUESTS

Lord, we ask that You would be made known to
those who have never heard about You.

We pray that once they hear of Your majesty, they would turn
from their sin and choose to follow You for all of their days.

We ask that they would let all that they are bring
You the praise You so rightly deserve.

We pray for the lost to be found.

In Jesus' name,

Amen

DAY 16

THE ULERICH FAMILY

All the paths of the LORD are steadfast love and faithfulness,
for those who keep his covenant and his testimonies.

Psalm 25:10 (ESV)

PRAISES

God, You are always with Your people.

You love Your people with a never-ending love.

You are unchanging.

Your plan for the nations, to have people from every nation and language worshipping You for eternity, has not changed.

When we follow Your ways, we will see Your love and faithfulness in our lives.

THANKS

God, thank You for the depth of your love for Your people. Before we knew that we needed You, You made a way for us to know You.

Thank You for your faithfulness, for Your constant care. Thank You for the way You are working in the world to bring people from every tribe, tongue, and nation into relationship with You.

REQUESTS

God, we pray for Your Word to be translated into every heart language.

Please raise up people to translate Your Word into their heart language.

Please work in the hearts of people groups who do not know You, so that when they hear about Your love in their heart language, they will hunger to know You and to follow You.

In Jesus' name,

Amen

DAY 17
THE FRAMES FAMILY

I am at rest in God alone;

my salvation comes from him.

He alone is my rock and my salvation,

my stronghold; I will never be shaken.

Psalm 62:1-2 (CSB)

PRAISES

God, You are our salvation.

You are our rock and the only place we will find rest.

In You, we can never be shaken.

THANKS

God, thank You that You are our only source
for salvation, and it is for all people.

Thank You that You desire to be a solid rock and
place of rest for those who have not heard Your Word
at all or do not have it in their heart language.

Thank You that because of your
salvation, we cannot be shaken.

REQUESTS

God, we pray that the message of Your salvation
will spread rapidly among the Bibleless.

We pray that they will know that You are the ONLY source
of salvation and that they can rest in your completed work.

Please give them the assurance of Your strength
and peace that in You they cannot be shaken.

You are their stronghold.

In Jesus' name,

Amen

DAY 18

THE NEWELL FAMILY

The LORD is my shepherd, I lack nothing.

He makes me lie down in green pastures,

he leads me beside quiet waters,

he refreshes my soul.

Psalm 23:1-3a (NIV)

PRAISES

God, You are merciful and full of compassion and lovingkindness.

You alone satisfy and sustain our needs.

You are perfect rest and peace; You are the right way and the only one worthy of praise.

THANKS

Thank You for calling and guiding missionaries to further Your kingdom.

Thank You for rest that restores our souls, for Your guidance in the way we should go.

Thank You for Your forgiveness, that we can glorify You with pure hearts.

REQUESTS

God, please instill contentment in the hearts of Your missionaries. Show them how You provide all their needs.

God, restore the souls and energy of Your missionaries so that they would wake each morning prepared for a new day of serving You.

God, bless the work of their hands that all they do would glorify You and point to You.

In Jesus' name,

Amen

DAY 19

THE BATES FAMILY

The LORD is gracious and righteous;

our God is compassionate.

The LORD guards the inexperienced;

I was helpless, and he saved me.

Psalm 116:5-6 (CSB)

PRAISES

God, we praise You for Your protection over Your beloved!

Even when we do not know or see the
enemy lurking, You are rescuing us.

Your righteousness never fails.

We praise You for the ways that You are moving
among and through Your people in every nation.

THANKS

Thank You, Father, for Your grace and righteousness.

You are so gracious with us.

Your grace and compassion overwhelm our weary
hearts and set our feet back on the rock.

Even in our most lonely place, our most shameful
secrets, even in our lowest moments, Your compassion
and righteousness meet us, and You rescue us
again and again! You are so good, Father.

Thank You for Your never-ending compassion.

REQUESTS

Father God, we lift up all of the missionaries and
pastors who are serving Your kingdom.

We ask that You would protect them from the enemy.

Help them to lift their weary hearts to You. We pray
that You would remind them of Your grace and
compassion in their lives over and over again.

In the name of Jesus, we pray that Your Holy Spirit will move
the hearts of the unreached to know You and to walk with You!

In Jesus' Name,

AMEN!

DAY 20

THE LOCHTE FAMILY

It is good to give thanks to the LORD,

to sing praises to the Most High.

It is good to proclaim your unfailing love in the morning,

your faithfulness in the evening.

Psalm 92:1-2 (NLT)

PRAISES

You are the Lord Most High.

God, You are WORTHY of praise in our songs, words, and actions.

God, You are always faithful.

THANKS

Thank You, Lord, for your never-ending faithfulness.

Thank You for loving and pursuing us endlessly.

Thank You for the gift of music to praise You and reach the hearts of so many.

REQUESTS

God Most High, may the pastors serving the Bibleless never cease to praise You for Your faithfulness.

God, may they always find joy in praising You from the time their eyes open in the morning until they close at night.

God, let the joy they have in praising and serving You be so contagious to fellow believers and unbelievers that they are encouraged to follow and praise You too!

In Jesus' name,

Amen

DAY 21

THE BRITTON FAMILY

The LORD protects his people,
and they can come to him
in times of trouble.
The LORD helps them
and saves them from the wicked
because they run to him.

Psalm 37:39-40 (CEV)

PRAISES

God, You are our protector, like a bodyguard in times of trouble.

You help us when we run to You.

You save us from the wicked.

THANKS

God, thank You for protecting translators around the world.

Thank You that they can run to You in times of trouble.

Thank You for helping Your people and saving them from the wicked.

REQUESTS

God, please continue to protect the many translators in dangerous areas of the world.

When they run to You in times of trouble, please help them.

When they call to You, save them from the wicked who want to stop the translation of Your mighty Word.

In Jesus' name,

Amen

DAY 22

THE LONG FAMILY

God Most High protects me like a shield.

He saves those whose hearts are right.

God judges by what is right.

And God is always ready to punish the wicked.

Psalm 7:10-11 (ICB)

PRAISES

God, You are my shield.

You save those whose hearts are true.

You are an honest judge.

THANKS

God, thank You for being a shield for pastors and protecting them from the ploys of the enemy.

Thank You for the salvation that You offer to all and for the pastors who share Your Gospel.

Thank You for being an honest judge who is holy and loving.

REQUESTS

God, please continue to shield and protect pastors and their families who serve You around the world.

Please allow them to see the fruit of their labor, with many receiving salvation.

Please allow them to see Your honest judgment as You protect them from any wickedness around them.

In Jesus' name,

Amen

DAY 23

THE LUJAN FAMILY

Who is this King of glory?

The LORD, strong and mighty,

the LORD, mighty in battle.

Psalm 24:8 (CSB)

PRAISES

God, You are the only one who is worthy of all glory!

Your might and strength are truly unmatched!

THANKS

God, thank You for our family and friends.

Thank You for fighting for us.

Thank You for giving us new brothers and sisters in our heavenly family.

REQUESTS

God, we pray for every child without the Bible in their heart language and without Yeshua in their lives to know You!

At the cross of Messiah You defeated all spiritual strongholds, so we pray for Your victory over every people group without any believers in You (Colossians 2:15)!

Confession: Heavenly Father, please forgive us for not caring more for people who still don't know Your love. Yeshua, help us to feel how You feel about people who still don't know about how You died for them!

In Jesus' name,

Amen

DAY 24

THE DSANE FAMILY

Why am I discouraged?
Why is my heart so sad?
I will put my hope in God!
I will praise him again —
my Savior and my God!

Psalm 42:5-6a (NLT)

PRAISES

God, You are our Savior.

You are gracious.

You are full of love.

You are with us when we are discouraged!

THANKS

God, thank You for uplifting the weary in Bible translation.

Thank You that You give the translators hope and strength to finish the work You have called them to.

We join them in praising You from all around the world.

We put our hope in You, and we thank You for being a good Father to us.

REQUESTS

God, please continue to encourage and strengthen the Bible translators, especially when they face discouragement and longsuffering.

Please help the workers to put their hope in You when the work becomes difficult.

In Jesus' name,

Amen

DAY 25

THE HAMILTON FAMILY

I love you, LORD God,
and you make me strong.
You are my mighty rock,
my fortress, my protector,
the rock where I am safe,
my shield,
my powerful weapon,
and my place of shelter.

Psalm 18:1-2 (CEV)

PRAISES

God, You are my protector.

You are mighty and all powerful.

You provide protection and a place of rest.

You are worthy of and victorious in all things.

THANKS

God, thank You for being a constant, mighty rock that missionaries stand on and draw strength from.

Thank You for shielding the missionaries from the attacks of the enemy.

Thank You for meeting each missionary right where they stand, sit, and lay, and for being their source of provision in whatever their needs may be.

REQUESTS

God, please continue to be a shelter for the missionaries who are walking in danger, needing a place to rest, or spiritually weary. Bring restoration.

God, please provide victory to missionaries all around the world as they work to grow Your kingdom.

In Jesus' name,

Amen

DAY 26

THE TUCKER FAMILY

But let all who take refuge in you rejoice;

let them shout for joy forever.

May you shelter them,

and may those who love your name boast about you.

For you, LORD, bless the righteous one;

you surround him with favor like a shield.

Psalm 5:11-12 (CSB)

PRAISES

God, You are our refuge, and we joyfully trust in You.

You are our shelter, and we proudly praise Your Name.

You are our shield of favor.

THANKS

God, thank You for being a refuge to the missionaries as they trust in Your plan to reach the lost.

Thank You for sheltering them as they share Your Name with those who do not know You.

Thank You for giving them a shield of favor, especially in unfriendly countries.

REQUESTS

God, please continue to give refuge to the missionaries as it becomes more dangerous to openly share the truth of Christ.

Please give the missionaries a shelter from the enemies that do not want them to proudly proclaim Your Name.

God, please give the missionaries favor in the hostile countries.

In Jesus' name,

Amen

DAY 27

THE KORDIC FAMILY

I have seen you in your sanctuary

and gazed upon your power and glory.

Your unfailing love is better than life itself;

how I praise you!

Psalm 63:2-3 (NLT)

PRAISES

Father, Your unmatched loving-kindness overwhelms us.

Your glory deserves all praise.

Your power is unrivaled.

You dwell on high.

THANKS

Father, thank You for the increasing number of people declaring Your love to unreached people.

Thank You that You make Yourself available in Your sanctuary.

Thank You for being a covenant-keeping God.

REQUESTS

Father, everybody without access to the Gospel needs to learn of Your power and glory.

May missionaries to unreached people groups truly love You as giver, and not just Your gifts.

Please direct the gaze of the unreached to Your Presence instead of idols.

In Jesus' name,

Amen

DAY 28

THE CRUM FAMILY

Lord God, you are my hope.
I have trusted you since I was young.

Psalm 71:5 (ICB)

PRAISES

God, You are our Lord.

You are our hope in tough times.

You are trustworthy and always have been.

THANKS

Thank You, God, for loving us from before birth.

Thank You for the hope found in Jesus' death and resurrection.

Thank You for faithful pastors who share
Your hope with the young (and old alike) who
have never experienced your Gospel.

REQUESTS

God, fill faithful pastors — working in unreached areas — who share Your hope and trust with the young, with the same hope and trust they know.

Bless their ministries, producing fruit
from the next generation.

Allow the childlike faith of the young to show adults true examples of pure faith, molding us all to be more like You.

In Jesus' name,

Amen

DAY 29

THE THURLING FAMILY

The LORD reigns! He is robed in majesty;
the LORD is robed, enveloped in strength.
The world is firmly established;
it cannot be shaken.
Your throne has been established
from the beginning;
you are from eternity.

Psalm 93:1-2 (CSB)

PRAISES

God, You are strong, and You are King of the World.

With Your strength we cannot be shaken,
no matter what happens around us.

THANKS

Thank You for being with every single person
in this world, especially those missionaries
who are reaching others for Your glory.

You are the same yesterday, today and forever; thank You
for your grand plan to establish Your Kingdom on this earth.

We are so grateful that we get the privilege
of telling others about You.

REQUESTS

Lord, please protect the missionaries all over
the world, especially in dangerous places.

Remind them that You are powerful and strong,
and that they can turn to You when they feel afraid
or overwhelmed, and You will protect them.

Give them the energy, enthusiasm, and courage to continue
to spread Your Word to every corner of the earth so that
everyone can know of Your great love and majesty.

Remind them that their peace comes from You,
knowing that You cannot be moved.

In Jesus' name,

Amen

DAY 30

THE HOLMSTROM FAMILY

O Lord, you are so good, so ready to forgive,
so full of unfailing love for all who ask for your help.

Psalm 86:5 (NLT)

PRAISES

God, You are such a good dad!

You are just waiting for us to turn to You so that
You can forgive us and lavish us with Your love.

You are ready to pour out Your help and love when we ask.

THANKS

God, thank You that You want everyone to know
You, and that You offer forgiveness and mercy
and grace to all who call on Your name!

Thank You that all we have to do is turn to You, and You
are ready to run toward us with Your loving arms.

REQUESTS

God, please continue to bring hope to the hopeless.

Help all those who don't know You cry out to You today, Lord.

Use even shame, sin, and addiction to turn
us toward You, our only hope!

Please hear the prayers of the broken, of those who
are depressed and anxious, of those who may have
lost touch with You or never knew You at all.

Help them to remember that You are quick
to offer help and forgiveness.

Scoop them up into Your loving arms, and fill them
with unfailing, never-ending love like only You can.

In Jesus' name,

Amen

DAY 31

THE CAMP FAMILY

Praise the Lord.

He alone is great.

He is greater than heaven and earth.

Psalm 148:13 (ICB)

PRAISES

God, You are our creator.

You created everything.

Creation declares Your power and glory.

You deserve our non-stop praise.

THANKS

God, thank You for creating new hearts
in us to know You and Your love.

Thank You for changing our hearts and opening our eyes.

Your power is able to change anyone; we know
this because You have changed us.

REQUESTS

God, please create a new heart in those
across the globe who don't know You.

Please give them a new heart, a new life, and a new hope.

Please give them hearts to know how much You love them.

In Jesus' name,

Amen

DAY 32

THE SMITH FAMILY

All you angels in heaven,
honor the glory and power
of the LORD!
Honor the wonderful name
of the LORD,
and worship the LORD
most holy and glorious.

Psalm 29:1-2 (CEV)

PRAISES

God, all glory and strength are Yours because of the splendor of Your holiness.

You speak, and all creation trembles.

THANKS

We thank You that You have created us in Your image and given us the ability to recognize Your glory and strength in creation.

REQUESTS

We ask that those across the globe who lift up false idols will see Your worth and ascribe to You the splendor due Your name.

May they join those who worship You according to these beautiful verses.

In Jesus' name,

Amen

DAY 33

THE COOTS FAMILY

The LORD will sustain him on his sickbed;
you will heal him on the bed where he lies.

Psalm 41:3 (CSB)

PRAISES

God, You are our healer and sustainer.

You visit the sick who are confined to their beds.

You are the Great Physician, the One in whom we trust.

THANKS

Lord, thank You for Your healing presence.

Thank You for hearing and answering prayers for pastors in faraway lands who are confined to sickbeds.

Thank You for Your mighty power to restore Christian workers and their families to health.

REQUESTS

Oh, God, our healer, draw close to global pastors who are ill or have sick family members.

Sustain them through pain, suffering, and despair.

Renew their resolve to follow You as they recover.

In Jesus' name,

Amen

DAY 34

THE ALLEN FAMILY

Where can I go to get away from your Spirit?
Where can I run from you?
If I go up to the skies, you are there.
If I lie down where the dead are, you are there.
If I rise with the sun in the east,
and settle in the west beyond the sea,
even there you would guide me.
With your right hand you would hold me.

Psalm 139:7-10 (ICB)

PRAISES

God, You are impossible to hide from.

You are in everything around us.

You are faithfully waiting for us to come home.

You are persistently calling us Yours.

THANKS

God, we thank You for guiding us throughout our life.

Thank You for making yourself known.

Thank You for being the light on our darkest days.

Thank You for never leaving us.

REQUESTS

God, we pray for those throughout the world who do not know Your love.

Please make Yourself known to the hearts that are broken so that they can find healing in You.

May Your Spirit fill them with an everlasting peace.

Lord, help Your believers among the unreached share the love of Jesus to those who do not know Him.

May they be able to show kindness and mercy, just as You have shown them.

In Jesus' name,

Amen

DAY 35

THE AXTENS FAMILY

But I will sing of your strength;

I will sing aloud of your steadfast love in the morning.

For you have been to me a fortress

and a refuge in the day of my distress.

Psalm 59:16 (ESV)

PRAISES

God, You are infinitely strong.

You love steadfastly.

God, You are our song.

You are our fortress and refuge.

THANKS

God, thank You for Your strength and love toward people who have never heard about Jesus.

Thank You for Your desire to hear songs from the lips of those who don't yet know Your son.

Thank You that You are a mighty fortress and refuge in our distress.

REQUESTS

God, we pray that You would put a beautiful melody in the hearts of the lost throughout the world.

May You make their hearts receptive to You.

Make a way for them to hear about and accept Jesus' gift of salvation so, with the redeemed, they can join in the song of Your strength and love.

We pray that You would reach out to them in their distress so they'll know You as a mighty fortress and refuge.

In Jesus' saving name and power,

Amen!

DAY 36

THE RITTENHOUSE FAMILY

The LORD is my strength and my shield;
my heart trusts in him, and I am helped.
Therefore my heart celebrates,
and I give thanks to him with my song.

Psalm 28:7 (CSB)

PRAISES

God, You are our strength and our protector.

You are trustworthy.

You are worthy of our thanksgiving and worship.

THANKS

Thank You for protecting pastors around the world.

Thank You for giving strength to pastors as they lead others to trust in You and sing songs of celebration and thanksgiving.

REQUESTS

Lord, protect and strengthen pastors in faraway lands who lead Your people. Please Help them to trust You more.

Please give them churches that are filled with celebration and thanksgiving.

In Jesus' name,

Amen

DAY 37

THE DRYDEN FAMILY

Our LORD, you are eternal!
Your word will last
as long as the heavens.
You remain faithful
in every generation,
and the earth you created
will keep standing firm.

Psalm 119:89-90 (CEV)

PRAISES

God, You are eternal!

You are faithful!

Your Word will last as long as the heavens!

THANKS

God, thank You for being faithful and giving missionaries strength and knowledge as they work on translating the Bible.

Thank You that the translated words of the Bible will last forever and always be true.

REQUESTS

God, please help the missionaries to persevere and remember that You will be faithful to help them.

Encourage them that their work of translating Your Word will last forever.

In Jesus' name,

Amen

DAY 38

THE MANCINELLI FAMILY

Your steadfast love, O LORD, extends to the heavens,

your faithfulness to the clouds.

Your righteousness is like the mountains of God;

your judgments are like the great deep;

man and beast you save, O LORD.

Psalm 36:5-6 (ESV)

PRAISES

God, Your love is bigger than the sky!

You always keep Your promises.

You are perfect, and You know everything.

You save us because of who You are!

THANKS

God, thank You that Your love goes further than those who can read the Bible in their own language, to every last person!

Thank You that You are faithfully revealing
Your glory to everyone.

Thank You for continually saving people all around the world.

REQUESTS

God, please make Your Word available to every last person in their own language, and please do it soon!

Please keep changing hearts, minds, and
lives with Your incredible love.

Please use Your Word to save them from
lies by washing them in truth.

By the power of Jesus,

Amen

DAY 39

THE TRAQUAIR FAMILY

> He heals the brokenhearted
> and bandages their wounds.
> He counts the stars
> and calls them all by name.
>
> Psalm 147:3-4 (NLT)

PRAISES

God, You are our great healer.

You are near the brokenhearted.

You know the number of stars in the sky.

You know the stars' names, and You know our names too.

THANKS

God, thank You for being near to the missionaries
who are far from home and suffer in many ways.

Thank You that You heal their physical and spiritual wounds.

Thank You for creating the stars in the sky, as they
remind our missionaries that You are their creator.

REQUESTS

God, please continue to heal Your
missionaries from their wounds.

Please cover them in Your mighty presence,
and let them know You are near.

Remind them daily that You not only know the names
of the stars, but You know their names personally.

In Jesus' name,

Amen

DAY 40
THE BENNETT FAMILY

Praise the Lord!

Praise God in his Temple.

Praise him in his mighty heaven.

Praise him for his strength.

Praise him for his greatness.

Psalm 150:1-2 (ICB)

PRAISES

God, You are worthy of all praise.

You are worthy of praise from everyone in every place.

You are mighty and strong.

You are altogether great.

THANKS

God, thank You that You have made everyone to praise You.

Thank You that You are stronger than any
power that could keep people from You.

Thank You that, in Your greatness, You are
making a way for everyone in every place to
be able to hear the truth about Jesus.

REQUESTS

God, please open the eyes of people across the
earth to see that they were made to praise You.

Please break every power that tries to
keep them from knowing You.

Please make a way, like only You can, for everyone in
every place to be able to hear the truth about Jesus.

In Jesus' Great Name,

Amen

LETTER OF GRATITUDE

Dear Prayer Contributors,

When I first had the idea to recruit families to each write a prayer for this book, part of me wondered if enough people could participate. I did not expect to have to turn away families because all of the spots were full!

I am incredibly thankful to the 40 families who gave their time and energy to write these wonderful prayers.

Your beautiful, Scripture-based prayers have inspired and challenged me, as I know they will many others.

You are a blessing to my family, and we pray this blessing over you:

> May the God of hope fill you with all joy and
> peace in believing, so that by the power of the
> Holy Spirit you may abound in hope.
>
> Romans 15:13 (ESV)

In Him,

Sarah

LIST OF CONTRIBUTORS

Frances and Mikel Allen — Pleasanton, Texas

Heather and Lee Axtens — Canton, Texas

Susannah and Jason Baker — Houston, Texas

Haley and Josh Bates — Poteet, Texas

Kriste and Scott Beavers — Boerne, Texas

Becky and Sean Bennett — Etna, Maine

Shannon and Jeff Britton — Rogersville, Missouri

Muffin and Morris Camp — San Antonio, Texas

Barbara and Gary Coots — Arlington, Texas

Jenny and Will Crum — Boerne, Texas

Amy and Will Dabney — Boerne, Texas

Julie and Dwaine Dement — Boerne, Texas

Sarah and Josh Deyton — Peachtree Corners, Georgia

Tammi and Chad Dryden — Zeeland, Michigan

Sky and Mike Dsane — Harbor City, California

Tamy and Jason Elam — Matthews, North Carolina

Wallis and Tyler Faught — Bang Khla, Thailand

Virginia and Michael Ferguson — Waco, Texas

Gwen and Ryan Frames — San Antonio, Texas

Kim and Weston Hamilton — Boerne, Texas

Sarah and Eric Holmstrom	Rancho Cucamonga, California
Lindsey and Kyle Johnson	College Station, Texas
Sarah and Ty Keeling	Boerne, Texas
Paula and Mark Kordic	Fort Worth, Texas
M'Rhea and Jason Lochte	Boerne, Texas
Jenn and Joel Long	Boerne, Texas
Kol and Solomon Lujan	Arlington, Texas
Loretta and Matt Mancinelli	Grosse Pointe Woods, Michigan
Stephanie and Shane Menn	Boerne, Texas
April and John Newell	Boerne, Texas
Holli and Scottye Perry	Arlington, Texas
Eileen and Scott Reaves	Boerne, Texas
Karen and Nate Rittenhouse	Williamsburg, Virginia
Kristi and Ryan Schmidt	Boerne, Texas
Laine and Jason Smith	Boerne, Texas
Steph and Jason Thurling	Excelsior, Michigan
Larissa and Bill Traquair	Boerne, Texas
Mandy and Brad Tucker	Rogersville, Missouri
Erin and Stephen Ulerich	French Camp, Mississippi
Lara and Lloyd Willis	Boerne, Texas

ABOUT THE AUTHOR

Sarah Keeling is passionate about helping others connect deeply with God. During difficult times, she developed a God-focused method of using Scripture to pray. She takes joy in sharing this method with both adults and children.

Sarah is an advocate and partner with Seed Company, a Bible translation organization focused on getting God's Word into every single native language across the earth.

She is the founder of Heart Work Tees, a T-shirt ministry that supported Bible translation.

As a young girl of 9, Sarah put her faith in Christ, but her journey didn't stop there. Debilitating chronic illness as an adult prompted her to dive deep into the Word of God for comfort and strength. Because of that experience, she now desires to share the hope God has given her with as many people as possible.

When her son developed a life-threatening illness, Sarah began using the Psalms to pray, and once again she experienced the incredible power of God's Word. She then taught her son how to pray the Psalms and saw his prayers transform as well.

Sarah wrote *Psalm Prayers for Kids: A 40-Day Prayer Journal* to help children learn how to pray the Psalms and experience transformation. It was published in 2019.

After her family used the Psalms to pray for friends in Oaxaca, Mexico, who are working in Bible translation, Sarah created *Psalm Prayers for the Nations* in 2020 to help other families participate in what God is doing around the world.

CHECK OUT SARAH'S PREVIOUS BOOK

PSALM PRAYERS FOR KIDS: A 40-DAY PRAYER JOURNAL

In this simple, easy-to-use prayer journal, Sarah explains how to teach your children an effective method to pray the Psalms. Your children will learn how to read a Psalm, identify the attributes of God, and then pray those attributes back to God through praise, thanks, and requests.

After personally praying the Psalms using this method, Sarah taught her son to pray this way too. She and her family members were amazed at the change it brought to her son's prayers. He was able to easily recall the attributes of God that he learned through praying the Psalms.

This book is a valuable resource to help your children connect deeply with God through praying His Word.

STAY CONNECTED!

FOR MORE FAMILY-FRIENDLY RESOURCES AND A FREE PRAYER GUIDE, VISIT

WWW.SARAH-KEELING.COM

www.ingramcontent.com/pod-product-compliance
Lightning Source LLC
Chambersburg PA
CBHW052105070526
44584CB00017B/2345